Psalms
for Single Parents

Psalms
for Single Parents

Collaborate Authors:

Minister Ardale Colhouer, Minister Lemuel Harris, Minister Ramon Thompson, Candace Edwards, Andrea Harris, Terica Marcellus, Reeshemah McCoy-Green, Elisabeth Lessey

XULON PRESS

Xulon Press
2301 Lucien Way #415
Maitland, FL 32751
407.339.4217
www.xulonpress.com

© 2018 Candace N. Edwards

All rights reserved solely by the author. The author guarantees all contents are original and do not infringe upon the legal rights of any other person or work. No part of this book may be reproduced in any form without the permission of the author. The views expressed in this book are not necessarily those of the publisher.

Unless otherwise indicated, Scripture quotations taken from the New King James Version (NKJV). Copyright © 1982 by Thomas Nelson, Inc. Used by permission. All rights reserved.

Printed in the United States of America.

ISBN-13: 978-1-54564-548-2

Table of Contents

Declaration: Psalm 115:11-18..........................vii
Exhortation: Fortitude................................ix

Chapter 1: Through the Fire and the Flood 1
Chapter 2: Rest in Jesus 4
Chapter 3: My Redeemer Lives 7
Chapter 4: Love Letters to Jesus.......................11
Chapter 5: In the Eyes of a Father 14
Chapter 6: God I Remember........................ 17
Chapter 7: The Fruit of Our Labor 22

A Prayer for Single Parents........................... 26
Helpful Resources................................... 28
A Heart of Gratitude (My Appreciation).................. 29
Reference Page 31

Declaration: Psalms 115:11-18

Ye that fear the LORD, trust in the LORD: he is their help and their shield. The LORD hath been mindful of us: he will bless us; he will bless the house of Israel he will bless the house of Aaron. He will bless them that fear the LORD, both small and great. The LORD shall increase you more and more, you and your children. Ye are blessed of the LORD which made heaven and earth. The heaven, even the heavens, are the LORD's: but the earth hath he given to the children of men. The dead praise not the LORD, neither any that go down into silence. But we will bless the LORD from this time forth for evermore. Praise the LORD!

Exhortation: Fortitude

*E*very parent, whether single or married, has experienced this word. Fortitude. This word is distinguished and authoritative. It's not a passive word. No, it's an aggressive and progressive word. It's an action word. Fortitude. Merriam-Webster online dictionary defines it as: "Strength of mind that enables a person to encounter danger or bear pain or adversity with courage." Fortitude. This is not a soft or comforting word. No, this is a hard word. Fortitude. We don't hear this word often, but instead we hear these words: strength, courage, grit, resiliency, stamina, determination, endurance and just plain guts.

As you look at these words, they all convey a message of pressing forward while experiencing pain, whether it's physical or emotional. Each single parent will experience their fair share of fortitude every day. Fortitude is taking a second job to put food on the table for your children. Fortitude is staying up all night with a sick child and having to call out of work the next day (without pay). Fortitude is teaching your children biblical principles consistently. Fortitude is fighting through the guilt and the shame of being a single parent, no matter how you became one. Fortitude is forgiving and covering the other parent in prayer even when you don't feel like it. It's retaking that class which you failed in order to get that degree. It's disciplining your child while you feel your heart breaking. It's finding the right kind of care for your special needs child. It's forsaking that bad habit in order to be a better example for your child and so much more.

Praise God for this word, fortitude, and its synonyms. If we have fortitude with Jesus, we are always victorious in the end because it is *He* who fortifies *us*. The book of Ecclesiastes 7:8 says the end of a matter is better than its beginning and patience is better than pride. Although the beginning of single parenting is hard, the end is better with Jesus.

Chapter One

Through the Fire and the Flood

Psalm 34:3-8

O magnify the LORD with me, and let us exalt His name together. I sought the LORD, and he heard me, and delivered me from all my fears. They looked unto him, and were lightened: and their faces were not ashamed. This poor man cried, and the LORD heard him, and saved him out of all his troubles. The angel of the LORD encampeth round about them that fear him, and delivereth them. O taste and see that the LORD is good: blessed is the man that trusteth in him.

I thank the Lord that I have a voice right now, to help others understand my process in walking with Christ as a single mother. I admit, in the beginning I did not want to be married but always knew I wanted children. Once I grew to understand that God loves marriage and His ways are always better, I accepted marriage and loved it. I learned to love what God loves and nothing on earth has helped me to seek and find Jesus more than single parenting. In my view, being a single parent is not always a bad thing. There is no telling what circumstance God will use to help a person grow. Over time, the Lord has revealed Himself to me in every part of my life in single parenthood. From the moment of conception— to every dark, rough, happy, and breakthrough moment, I became closer to Jesus. Just when I thought I knew everything and I was in control, Jesus showed me whose boss. In fact, He showed me that He is the *MASTER* and He loves me. I mean when things got rough, scary, unbearable, and unbelievable I got out of the boat and walked with Jesus.

I've been homeless twice, and even lived in a shelter once while carrying my first child at 20 years old. While I was there, I gave my life to Christ. It was a long road of Christian maturity for me so you can say that my kids and I grew up together. At that time, I was a high school dropout and in an abusive relationship. Jesus turned it all around and He turned the tables on the devil. God opened doors to opportunities, which gave me the confidence I needed to keep moving forward. I graduated college with a Paralegal and Bachelor degree from the University of South Florida and later also a degree in ministry. The Lord has blessed me with a brand new home for me and my 3 children. Truth be told, things didn't become any easier for me because the Lord is in my life. I just dealt with it better by choosing to keep a grateful and positive attitude. Desperately wanting to be loved and accepted, I attracted the wrong attention in men and friends.

I wanted to speak but I chose silence instead and it empowered my oppressors. I even found myself in a marriage with a crack addict. Many times my kids and I were under demonic attacks and faced dangerous situations, including poverty. I learned to praise my way through and I remember crying on the floor because I was so tired of struggling. I was in so much pain from being lied to and I felt so helpless. My husband at the time, had stolen a lot of money and I had back surgery so I couldn't work and I didn't have anyone to turn to. All I had was $25.00 and a business card from an idea that I had. I prayed and cried out to the Lord. The Holy Spirit made Himself so real to me in a tangible way. He wrapped His arm around me, it felt like a wonderful blanket and He told me to throw down the money like Moses threw down his shepherd rod. In other words, God wanted me to sow it into His Kingdom. He wanted me to trust Him with my last idea and my last dollars. So I did what He asked and when I picked it back up I had a thriving business that paid all my bills and then some. I never wanted for nothing after that. Not only that, Jesus gave me a voice. He made me relevant to the City of Tampa.

My daughter Legacy and I are working with the mayor to help our community in Sulphur Springs. Right now I am ministering the gospel, own a business, living in my brand new home, my son is the head musician in church and my daughter is singing lead in the kids choir, and soon we will expand the gospel through our own radio show. The best is yet to come because the Lord is faithful. I would tell single parents that there will always be something that will try to disturb your stability, so forgive quickly. Somethings in life you have no control over and your intelligence is not enough for you to figure a way out. I encourage you to seek God's way, stand on His Word, and walk in faith. Pay your tithes and sow greatly and praise Him in spirit and in truth, it invites Him into any situation. The healing is understanding that your voice is powerful, so use it wisely and often speaking the Word of God over yourself and your child/children's lives and denying the devil access.

As a single parent, I can say that I was in over my head and all I could do was believe that in JESUS, I can do all things, and I can do it *through* Him. Although, my circumstances told me I couldn't make it and I had failed times *BEFORE*. The fear of what could happen brought many emotional strongholds that I had to overcome. I always have to remember my past blessings and miracles. I had to speak success and press through. I don't doubt that God can do amazing things for others, but in my personal crisis I had to believe the ultimate human experience...Resurrection power. My faith elevated me to a great height and it is very good.

Daniel 11:32b-But the people who know their God shall be strong and carry out great exploits.

John 16:33 King James Version (KJV)

~Reeshemah McCoy-Green

Chapter Two

Rest in Jesus

Psalm 127:1-2

Except the LORD build the house, they labour in vain that build it: except the LORD keep the city, the watchman waketh but in vain. It is vain for you to rise up early, to sit up late, to eat the bread of sorrows: for so he giveth his beloved sleep.

My mother use to tell me this old adage which still sticks with me to this day "being a mother is not for the faint at heart." Boy, was she ever right. I have been on this mothering journey for almost 11 years now, and it has been action packed since day one. From changing diapers to being a soccer/football mom, nurse, mediator, chauffer, cook and everything else in between, I am always on the go. It's only a season I know, but it's hard for me to just relinquish control as a parent. Yes, I admit it! When you're a single parent and you know there are little people who are totally dependent on you (for now), it can cause a great deal of anxiety and uncertainty, especially living in this chaotic world. When I first became a single parent I went through a season where I truly learned what it meant to live by the grace and mercy of God. He had to teach me how to transition from being a wife to being a single parent and the struggle was REAL folks! Through that time, God kept me in the midst of the rough seasons of parenting and allowed me to stay in my right mind (most of the time anyway).

My goal as a parent is to raise my children to love Jesus and have a personal relationship with Him, while provoking them to be a godly influence for their generation. As great as this goal is, I know I can't do it alone. God uses the body of Christ to step in and come along side me while I raise them. I remember one night the youth pastor of our local church was preaching to the congregation. He testified that even though he was raised in the church and his mother taught him truth, he still decided to live in the world. He would go to parties and get into mischief; however, what his mother didn't know was there were times that he and a friend would sit down and actually read the bible! This caused for a 10 seconds praise break!

What his mother didn't know was God was dealing with her son's heart even though it didn't look it. This young man is *now* preaching the gospel and I am encouraged, after hearing his testimony mainly for three reasons. 1. I was also a rebellious child and *now* here I am serving the Almighty God. 2. This young preacher was the fruit of his mother's labor. 3. If my children decide to go their own way outside of God's will, He can still work in their lives without my presence. The brutal reality is I'm raising two children who could possibly go down the same road I did. I don't know what they will face as they get older…but God does. I don't know who they will encounter when I am not around… but God does and He has their lives in His hands. That assurance is comforting and it gave my heart rest. Not only that, it allowed me to actually enjoy who my children are. I see the gifts that God placed in their lives and He is able to make them manifest in His time and for His purpose.

The season which I'm in right now is to rest in Him and trust Him with my children. Honestly, it's a scary thing for me and I have always found counsel and encouragement from older women who lived it not perfectly, but victoriously. I can't wait to see what God has in store for my children and to see the fruit of my labor. God promised me that He will help me train and raise them, He will make up the difference where I'm lacking, and He knows what we need as a family more than I do. Another goal of mine as a single parent, is to leave a godly legacy for my children to put their trust in God. When they are grown and have families of their own, I want them to testify that I was a faithful woman of God. When it's all said and done, I want to hear the words "Well done, thy good and faithful servant."

~Candace N. Edwards

Chapter Three

My Redeemer Lives

Psalm 34:19-22

Many are the afflictions of the righteous: but the LORD delivereth him out of them all. He keepeth all his bones: not one of them is broken. Evil shall slay the wicked: and they that hate the righteous shall be desolate. The LORD redeemeth the soul of his servants: and none of them that trust in him shall be desolate.

Marriage is a big commitment. We think it's easy and it's about love and living in paradise. In 2001, I decided to separate from my husband. My mother-in-law lived with us for 13 years and it was not an easy road. I believe the number one priority in a home is putting God first and then your immediate family. Looking back on it now, there was a lot of verbal and physical abuse and it wasn't good for my two sons. There was no peace or joy in my home and I didn't have any family close to me at the time. My mother lived in Panama and was ill with an enlarged heart. One day after an argument with my husband, I decided to pick up my Bible and turned to:

Psalm 27:1-4:
The LORD is my light and my salvation; whom shall I fear?
The LORD is the strength of my life; of whom shall I be afraid?

When the wicked, even mine enemies and my foes came upon me to eat up my flesh, they stumbled and fell.

Though an host should encamp against me, my heart shall not fear: though war should rise against me, in this will I be confident. One thing have I desired of the LORD, that I may dwell in the house of the LORD all the days of my life, to behold the beauty of the LORD, and to enquire in his temple.

Psalms 31:3-4
For thou art my rock and my fortress; therefore for thy name's sake lead me, and guide me. Pull me out of the net that they have laid privily for me: for thou art my strength.

In this generation, I don't believe we have a true understanding that marriage is for better, worse, sickness, health, poverty, and wealth. If we are not careful we can get married for the wrong reasons and the children are the ones who are greatly affected. I admit I was guilty of this because I never prayed to God about it. I wanted it my way and I fought the battle alone. I went to church but I didn't put my faith in God about my situation.

Psalm 46:1, 10-11
God is our refuge and strength, a very present help in trouble. Be still and know that I am God: I will be exalted among the heathen, I will be exalted in the earth.

At the time, I wanted a husband that shared his love, thoughts, friendship, kindness, and humbleness with me. But, my God was telling me He is my Creator, He owns everything and that He will take care of me despite what I going through. My sons were not doing well in school and I began to lose weight. Once I was able to get child support, I moved out of my home and in with a distant cousin for three years. Things got even worse and I believed this is one of the worst things I had done. You see when you do not allow God into your life bad things will happen.

Psalm 25:16-18
Turn thee unto me, and have mercy upon me; for I am desolate and afflicted. The troubles of my heart are enlarged: O being thou me out of my distresses. Look upon mine affliction and my pain; and forgive all my sins.

Those three years I lived with my cousin was not easy, but no matter what I was going through, I never gave up on God. I prayed that God would deliver me one day. My prayer was answered in 2004, and I was able to move out of the state of New York. However, on September 11, 2004, my mother passed away and on October 23, 2004 my two sons and I were released to move to Florida.

Psalms 34:1-4
I will bless the LORD at all times: his praise shall continually be in my mouth. My soul shall make her boast in the LORD: the humble shall hear thereof, and be glad.

Once I moved to Florida, I was baptized in October 2004 and filled with the Holy Ghost in March 2005. My oldest son Aurelio was baptized and received the Holy Ghost in December 2004. My youngest son, Stefon was baptized in 2006 during a youth revival service. At the time, being a single mother was not easy. It was very hard for me to raise two boys and I only instructed them as a mother, to the best of my ability. I attended New Life Tabernacle and met other single mothers like myself and we are friends still to this day. Prayer is the answer. As our children grew, we prayed daily for them. I have been through a lot as a single parent. Job loss, multiple car accidents, surgery, health issues, and homelessness, but God was faithful to me. In 2013 my divorce was final.

Psalm 73:18-19
Surely thou didst set them in slippery places: thou castedst them down into destruction. How are they brought into desolation, as in a moment! They are utterly consumed with terrors.

Psalm 91:14-16
Because he hath set his love upon me, therefore will I deliver him: I will set him on high, because he hath known my name. He shall call upon thee, and I will answer him: I will be with him in trouble; I will deliver him and honour him. With long life will I satisfy him, and shew my salvation.

Psalm 100:1-5
Make a joyful noise unto the LORD, all ye lands. Serve the LORD with gladness: come before his presence with singing. Know ye that the LORD he is God: it is he that hath made us and not we ourselves; we are his people, and the sheep of his pasture. For the LORD is good; his mercy is everlasting and his truth endureth to all generations.

In this life, all of us will face disappointment until we see the New Jerusalem. We must continue to pray for our children and the next generation to come. This world will not get better. We need to be reminded to focus on the plan of God. His Son, Jesus, is coming soon. We need to stop wasting our minds on the past and focus on what God wants from us now. It's not easy to be a single parent, but ask God for direction and He will guide your path. We must be righteous and holy in what we do for God. Pray for the salvation for those who do us wrong. It is a healing process so focus on Jesus. Today, both of my sons are serving the Lord and I am a grandmother of two.

Psalm 118:28-29
Thou art my God, and I will praise thee: thou art my God, I will exalt thee. O give thanks unto the LORD; for he is good: for his mercy endureth forever.

~ Elisabeth Lessey

Chapter Four

Love Letters to Jesus

Lord,
Right now my mouth cannot form the words to tell
You how great Thou art.
But my heart speaks of Your tender mercies which are
renewed daily.
I am constantly reminded of Your love for me
And I yearn to speak with my lips of Your beauty and Your grace.
Even in the midst of a storm, I can see Your sweetness.
I can feel Your tenderness when the wind passes.
I hear Your whispers of love. Almighty God,
You are my Comforter,
You are my Protection, my Peace,
My Joy, my Salvation comes from You.
What more can I do but praise You?
Not for anything that You have done for me materially,
but just because You Are.

Written by Terica Marcellus

Psalms for Single Parents

Psalm 25

Show me, teach me, lead me
Your ways, Your paths, Your truth.
Teach me God, my Savior, my Lord
All day will I wait on You.
Remember, Lord Your mercies, Your love
For they have always been.
When I was a child, I spake as a child.
Remember not my sins
For Your goodness sake remember me
Good and upright art Thou.
You teach us in Your ways,
You guide is in Your judgements
And to be meek You teach us how
All Your paths are mercy and truth.
To those that keep Your Word
For Your name's sake pardon our sins
Make us to inherit the earth.

Written by Terica Marcellus

This Love

This love is a perfect love,
It casts out every fear.
This love is pure and holy,
It cleanses every smear.
Unconditional love
That's what God is
For when I was a slave to sin
He came to make me His.
I've never known such love so sweet;
I thought that I had searched everywhere,
But just when I had lost all hope
He let me know that He was there.
This love is a perfect love,
Tears of sorrow no longer I cry.
This love is pure and holy,
It brings righteousness, joy, and peace of mind.

Written by Terica Marcellus

Chapter Five

In the Eyes of a Father

Psalm 16

*P*reserve *me, O God: for in thee do I put my trust. O my soul, thou hast said unto the LORD, Thou art my Lord: my goodness extendeth not to thee; But to the saints that are in the earth, and to the excellent, in whom is all my delight. Their sorrows shall be multiplied that hasten after another god: their drink offerings of blood will I not offer, nor take up their names into my lips. The LORD is the portion of mine inheritance and of my cup: thou maintains my lot. The lines are fallen unto me in pleasant places, yea, I have a goodly heritage. I will bless the LORD, who hath given me counsel: my reins also instruct me in the night seasons. I have seen the LORD always before me: because he is at my right hand, I shall not be moved. Therefore my heart is glad, and my glory rejoiceth: my flesh also shall rest in hope. For thou wilt not leave my soul in hell; neither wilt thou suffer thine Holy One to see corruption. Thou wilt shew me the path of life: in thy presence is fullness of joy, at thy right hand there are pleasures for evermore.*

Psalm 42
As the dear panteth after the water brooks, so panteth my soul after thee, O God. My soul thirsteth for God, for the living God: when

shall I come and appear before God? My tears have been my meat day and night, while they continually say unto me, Where is thy God? When I remember these things, I pour out my soul in me: for I had gone with the multitude, I went with them to the house of God, with the voice of joy and praise, with a multitude that kept holy day. Why art thou cast down, O my soul? And why art thou disquieted in me? Hope thou in God: for I shall yet praise him for the help of his countenance. O my God, my soul is cast down within me: therefore will I remember thee from the land of Jordan, and of the Hermonites, from the hill Mizar. Deep calleth unto deep at the noise of thy waterspouts: all thy waves and thy billows are gone over me. Yet the LORD will command his lovingkindness in the daytime, and in the night his song shall be with me, and my prayer unto God of my life. I will say unto God my rock, why hast thou forgotten me? Why go I mourning because of the oppression of the enemy? As with a sword in my bones, mine enemies reproach me; while they say daily unto me, where is thy God? Why art thou cast down, O my soul? And why art thou disquieted within me? Hope thou in God: for I shall yet praise him, who is the health of my countenance, and my God.

Although we realize that the majority of single parents are mostly mothers, we applaud the efforts, strength, and courage single fathers contribute in raising godly children. Their guidance can help direct and encourage single fathers on being the solo leaders God has called them to be in their home.

What encouragements can you give single fathers in how to raise godly children?

There are a few things that helped me during this hard period:
1. I stayed faithful in the House of God.
2. I talked with my Pastor for the best advice on how to deal with frustrations and anger. I didn't always apply what he said and as a result, I felt the effect of it every time.
3. One major thing that encouraged me was seeing other brothers going through the same thing and them turning to me for advice. They were inspired by how I handled my

situation and were challenged to see if they had the strength to make it through their situation.

What are the struggles single fathers may face?

1. Time management. Because the time I have with my son is limited, it's hard trying to find a balance so I can spend the time I would like with him. Children need their fathers, not only to know them but also to spend time with them.
2. Loneliness. This was one of my biggest struggles. Many times, I would pray for a helpmeet. I wanted someone who could help when my son was sick or stayed home with him while I run to get medicine. It was especially hard when we went to the park and seen families that were complete.

Is there a scripture from the book of Psalms, which helped you in your period of single parenting?

1. Psalms 16 and Psalms 42

It helps to remember where you come from, past battles the Lord has brought you through, and to refocus on where you're headed.

~Minister Ramon Thompson

An informal interview was done by an anonymous brother at our local church, who was formally a single father of a daughter. He was asked what types of advice he would give to fathers who are raising daughters. He briefly listed 4 things:

1. You must realize that you can't raise a daughter by yourself. The daughter needs to be around other godly women.
2. Fathers can be very protective of their daughters and the influences around them. Keep your daughters out of drama as much as possible.
3. When thinking about marrying a woman, find a woman who has a quality that your daughter will need. (i.e. punctuality, good attitude, etc.)
4. As the father, you must be firm and consistent with your daughter.

~Anon

Chapter Six

GOD I REMEMBER...

Psalm 103:2-6

Bless the LORD, O my soul: and all that is within me, bless his holy name. Who forgiveth all thine iniquities; who healeth all thy diseases; Who redeemeth thy life from destruction; who crowneth thee with lovingkindness and tender mercies; Who satisfieth thy mouth with good things; so that thy youth is renewed like eagel's. The LORD executeth righteousness and judgment for all that are oppressed.

GOD I REMEMBER...
As a single parent, I remember going to my prenatal appointments alone while I was still married.

I remember shopping at the WIC store with both of my children.

I remember buying diapers, wipes, and formula for my daughter.

I remember cutting my own grass with my friend's lawn mower.

I remember taking my children to multiple counseling and doctor appointments.

I remembered receiving financial assistance from Catholic Charities while I was pregnant.

I remember taking my children to different schools to eat free breakfast and lunch because I didn't have any food in my home.

I remember church members bought groceries for us, because I ran out of money at the end of each month.

I remember grocery shopping through the snow and having to bundle my children up.

I remember pursuing a bachelor's degree while I was pregnant with my daughter and walking across the stage to graduate when she was 5 months old.

I remember moving to Florida and attending the University of South Florida for my Master's degree and having to start over from scratch because none of my other credits transferred.

I remember keeping my daughter for a whole school year because I could not afford childcare.

I remember going to more food banks because I did not qualify for food stamps or childcare subsidy.

GOD I REMEMBER…
I remembered that through all those obstacles, You strengthened me when I wanted to give up.

I remember how You comforted me when I needed a blood transfusion.

I remember how You comforted me when I cried all night because of the failures and the disappointments I faced.

I remember how You opened doors for me that I could not open for myself.

I remember how You blessed me to be a homeowner at the age of 32.

I remember how You blessed me to publish my first book at the age of 32, my second at 34, and now my third at 35.

I remember how You gave me glimpses of hope and rewards of parenting and the seeds that are being sown.

I remember how You provided clothes for myself and my children.

I remember how You protected us from the unrelenting struggles of this life.

I remember that You called me Your beloved when I felt like everything but loved.

I remember how You have given me unspeakable joy in times of sorrow.

GOD I STILL DO REMEMBER...

~ Candace N. Edwards

Chapter Seven

The Fruit of Our Labor

Psalm 127:3-5

Lo, children are an heritage of the LORD: and the fruit of the womb is his reward. As arrows are in the hand of a mighty man; so are children of the youth. Happy is the man that hath his quiver full of them: they shall not be ashamed, but they shall speak with the enemies in the gate.

To begin, let me say that growing up without my dad in the home was very rough. You see, my dad and mom divorced when I was around 8 years old. I often hoped, longed for, eagerly waited for the day that he would return. Much to my dismay, that day never came. It seemed as though I was destined to grow up in the inner city of Miami, without the guidance of my dad. Fortunately, I was blessed with an amazing mom. She worked extremely hard to care for, provide for, and raise my sister and me. Although there are several things that I could list that demonstrated my mom's tireless efforts to make my life better and productive, there are a few that stood out the most.

One of the things I appreciated the most was my mom's demonstration of what it means to work hard, yet be there for your family. My mom worked two, sometimes three jobs, at any given time. Everyone in my school knew my mom and it was rare that she missed any of my basketball games. She would volunteer for my field trips and made herself available to communicate with my teachers (whether I wanted her to or not). My mom also made sure that we went on memorable family vacations. I vividly remember the fishing trips my mom took us on and the walks around the neighborhood, in which I would collect odd trinkets along the way. I will always be grateful to my mother for sacrificing her time to me and my family. Another thing that stands out in my mind about my mom was her distinctive virtue. I have never seen my mom with any man, other than my dad. She never remarried, yet remained pristine in my eyes.

While I can only imagine how difficult it was for her, this is something that has made me hold my mom in high respect for years. Lastly, the best thing my mom did for me was just trying to be a good mom. She did not try to take the place of my dad; she simply did all that she could to be a great mom. My mom was patient, loving, nurturing, consistent disciplinarian, hardworking, honest and forthcoming. She would take me out of our neighborhood and show me that there was life outside of what I saw every day. This gave me vision and freed me from the mental boundaries in which many young men found themselves. With the help of God and my mom, I graduated college, became an HR Manager, began my own business, became a licensed minister, and have been blessed to pastor a great church for a year. I thank God for placing me in the care of such a mom. While I am not as great a man as my mom is a woman, I do have in her a goal to strive towards.

~Minister Lemuel Harris

Chapter Eight

The Fruit of our Labor Continued...

Psalm 121

I will lift up mine eyes unto the hills, from whence cometh my help. My help cometh from the LORD, which made heaven and earth. He will not suffer thy foot to be moved: he that keepeth thee will not slumber. Behold, he that keepeth Israel shall neither slumber nor sleep. The LORD is thy shade upon thy right hand. The sun shall not smite thee by day nor the moon by night. The LORD shall preserve thee from all evil: he shall preserve thy soul. The LORD shall preserve thy going out and thy coming in from this time forth, and even for evermore.

My son's father and I married on September 26, 1973. At the time, I was approaching twenty years old and erroneously assumed that I was so much older and wiser. In fact, I was clueless; clueless that my husband had broken rank with the generation preceding him. He graduated from high school under duress and after a stint in the military, he enrolled in Control Data Institute, where he graduated and took a job in cutting edge technology. My ex-husband built computer boards. He built them during work hours and he built them in his sleep. He had no frame of family reference on how to function in corporate America. In all honesty, I did not know how to be a wife and he was a decent man, who did not understand how to be a husband. Thus my bright, inquisitive, sensitive, and athletic son grew up without a father in our home alongside his bright, sensitive, inquisitive, wired for the theater sister.

Three Things I know I did well:

1) I prayed
2.) I prayed
3.) I prayed

Three Things I wish I had done better:

1) Listened more to my beloved children and talked much less.
2) Found more reasons to laugh out loud with my beloved children.
3) Spent more time with my beloved children.

Things I suggest to single parents:

1) Pray!
2) Stay connected with the absent parent if it is not unsafe or toxic. If you just no longer can stand him or her; it happens, parent-up; deal with it maturely. ***It's not about you.***
3) Listen, laugh, and spend time with your beloved children.
4) Pray more.

~Sister Andrea Harris (Minister Lemuel Harris' mother)

Psalm 31
In thee, O LORD, do I put my trust; let me never be ashamed: deliver me in thy righteousness.

It was two weeks before Easter Sunday 1992. I was stationed at Fort Polk, Louisiana. I had just given my son a bath and was trying to lay him down to sleep. I was tired, he was fed, he was dry, and he wouldn't stop crying. Suddenly a rage like I've never felt before in my life came over me. A voice in my mind said to throw him against the wall. I was mortified that I would think to do such a thing. As I held him in my hands, my elbows locked, I turned slowly and laid him in his crib. I went to my bedroom across from his and knelt at my bed. I began to cry and tell God that I didn't want to be an abusive parent like my mother and stepfather. I vowed to God that if he would help me be a good mother, I would serve him.

On April 19, 1992 I went to a storefront non-denominational Pentecostal church that was pastored by a sergeant in my unit. Six weeks later, on April 31st, a visiting United Pentecostal Church preacher preached that Sunday morning about receiving the Holy Ghost and the day of Pentecost. The week prior I had repented of my sins and received prayer for deliverance of a stronghold which had me bound since my childhood. After the deliverance, I tried to receive the Holy Ghost and cried out to God in praise. All I could muster was a "hah." This Sunday was different. As the visiting preacher's wife prayed for me, I felt the love of God wash over me, and I felt His peace. I became afraid and the preacher's wife must have sensed it and said, "Don't be afraid, He is a gentleman." I then relaxed and the "hah, hah" began again. She said, that's it; that is the Holy Ghost!" Immediately the instant I had faith to believe, the "Hah" became "Hallelujah" and I began to speak in tongues and jump so high.

I was filled with joy, because He accepted me, a 32-year-old sinner like me. After being filled with the Holy Ghost I began to read the word of God with understanding. The Lord, through the Holy Ghost, began to reveal the oneness of God to me through the scriptures. Specifically, we receive the Spirit of adoption whereby we cry ABBA Father, and if you have not the Spirit of Christ you are none of his. I told my pastor that I would be attending the UPC church, because I believed the way they believed, according to the Bible. A short while later, I was at home reading the book of Samuel and I related to Hanna's plight. I was told by a doctor that it would be hard for me to conceive, but despite what man said, the Lord had blessed me with a child. After reading Samuel, I begin to bless my son and dedicate him to the Lord. I blessed his intellect, character and his future.

~Minister Ardale Colhouer

A Prayer for Single Parents

Heavenly Father,

*Y*ou are the Creator of heaven and earth, and You are sovereign in all of Your ways. You are the most high God and there is no one like You. LORD, we come before You thanking You for choosing us to nurture and train the next generation of disciples for Your glory and Your purpose. Father, we do not take this task lightly and we realize that we need Your help. We cannot do anything apart from You. LORD, You said in Your word that we are to train up a child in the way they should go and when they become old they will not depart from it. Father, watch over the seeds that have been planted in their lives while they are under our care. You know every test, trial, and temptation they will face in the future. Father, we ask that You will give them the boldness to stand firm in their faith and that they will not sell their godly inheritance. We know the thief comes to steal and to kill, and to destroy but You have come that we all might have life and have it more abundantly. O LORD, we plead the blood of Jesus against every attack, plan, distraction, and deceptive work that the enemy has for our children's destruction. We speak life over them and that no weapon formed against them will be able to prosper. They will fulfill the divine purpose that You have ordained over their lives, before the foundation of the world.

A Prayer for Single Parents

Father, we ask that You send a fresh anointing over us who are single parents. LORD, give us wisdom on how to raise our children to love and reverence You. LORD, provide the resources that we will need to successfully raise our children. Remind us, O LORD that You are with us and You will never forsake us. We will put our trust in You and we will be of good courage because this is Your will concerning us in this season. Strengthen us as parents LORD, because we look to You for help. You are our banner, our provider, our protector, our healer, our friend, our counselor, our comforter, and our Father. Let us see the fruit of our labor when our children are older, knowing that our labor is not vain. We thank You LORD for where You have brought us from and we thank You for where You are taking us. May we deepen our relationship with You. We love You and we honor You Father, not only for what You have done but for who You are. In the mighty name of Jesus. Amen.

Helpful Resources

The Five Language of Children by Dr. Gary Chapman & Dr. Ross Campbell

- Bringing Up Girls: *Practical Advice and Encouragement for Those Shaping the Next Generation of Women* by Dr. James Dobson
- *The New Strong-Willed Child* by Dr. James Dobson
- Prayers for Prodigals: *90 Days of Prayer for Your Child* by James Banks https://www.thespruce.com/single-parent-ministries-2998104.
- Raise Him Up*: A Single Mother's Guide to Raising a Successful Black Man* by Derrick and Stephanie Moore
- Book of Prayers: *The Power of a Praying Parent* by Stormie Omaritan
- *Raising Men not Boys* by Mike Fabarez

A Heart of Gratitude (My Appreciation)

Wow! Creating a collaborative book has been a faith stretcher for me and I am so grateful to God for this vision that He has entrusted me with. I am grateful that He has provided the means and opportunities for this work to be accomplished for His glory and for the strengthening of His people. Thank you LORD. Next, I want to thank Orlando and Teryka Haynes for their divine gift of trailblazing. I came to you with a vision and you pointed me in the right direction. Thank you. I want to thank all of the authors who poured their memories and testimonies in order to encourage the generations behind them. Those seasons were not in vain. Thank you Sharon Taylor for your patience and your gift of creativity with the cover design. Last, but certainly not least, the readers of this book. I pray that this has blessed you along the way of parenting and you are encouraged because of it. God bless you and your family.

Reference Page

King James Version Bible Pocket Edition Copyright © 2016 by Christian Art Publishers P.O. Box 1599, Vereeniging, 1930, RSA
https://www.merriam-webster.com/

https://www.census.gov/library/visualizations/2016/comm/cb16-192_living_arrangements.html

Book Graphic Designs created by Sharon Taylor

www.ingramcontent.com/pod-product-compliance
Ingram Content Group UK Ltd.
Pitfield, Milton Keynes, MK11 3LW, UK
UKHW022218230426
12048UKWH00016BA/917